How To Grow Onions
With Notes on Onion Varieties

by Tuisco Greiner and Col. C.H. Arlie

with an introduction by Roger Chambers

Self Reliance Books

Get more historic titles on animal and stock breeding, gardening and old fashioned skills by visiting us at:

http://selfreliancebooks.blogspot.com/

Introduction

I am pleased to present yet another title on Gardening.

The work is in the Public Domain and is re-printed here in accordance with Federal Laws.

As with all reprinted books of this age that are intended to perfectly reproduce the original edition, considerable pains and effort had to be undertaken to correct fading and sometimes outright damage to existing proofs of this title. At times, this task is quite monumental, requiring an almost total "rebuilding" of some pages from digital proofs of multiple copies. Despite this, imperfections still sometimes exist in the final proof and may detract from the visual appearance of the text.

I hope you enjoy reading this book as much as I enjoyed making it available to readers again.

Roger Chambers

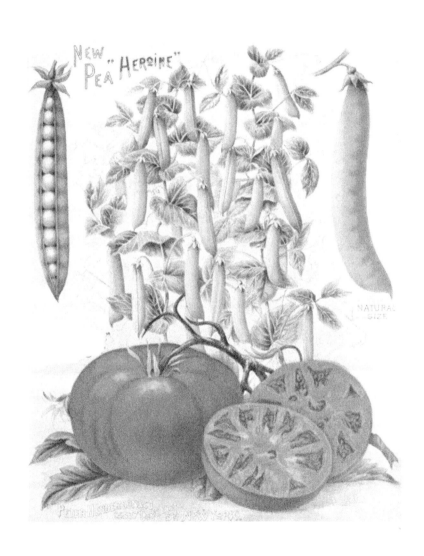

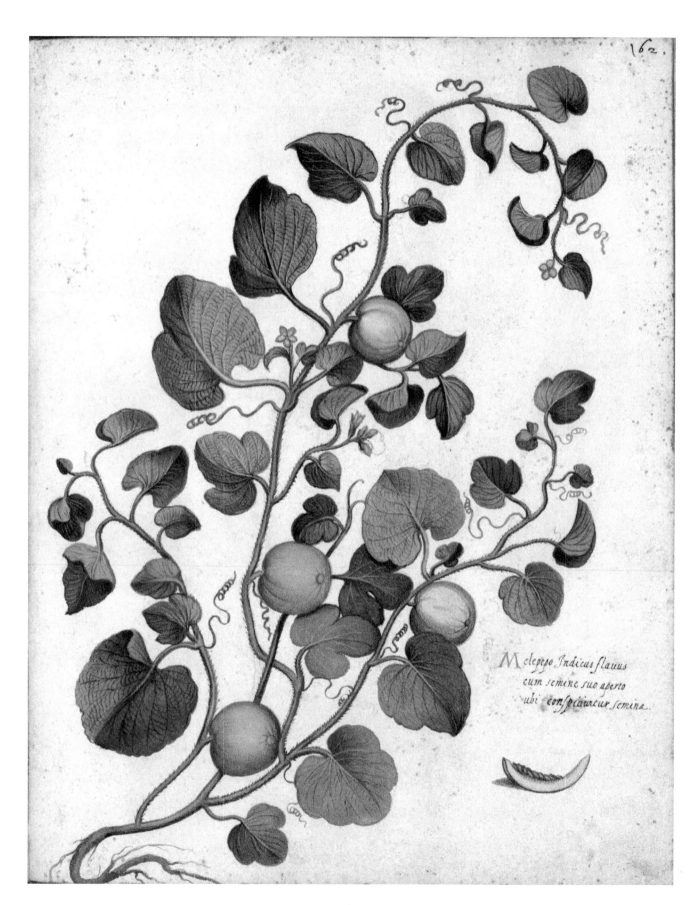

Melepepo Indicus flauus
cum semine suo aperto
ubi conspeciuntur semina.

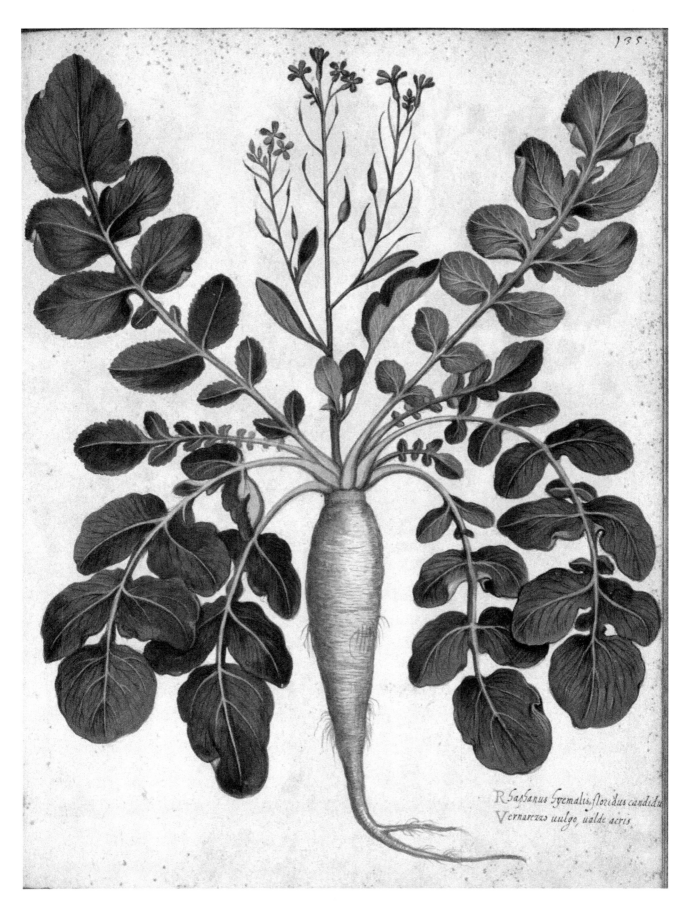

R.Saphanus hyemalis, floridus candidus
Vernarezzo uulgo, ualde acris.

R *apum rotundum album et pur*
N *auone uulgo n.° 1.*
R *apum rotundum albun*
N *auone Bianco n.° 2.*

CONTENTS.

CONTENTS.

EDITOR'S PREFACE.

The offer in BURPEE'S FARM ANNUAL FOR 1887, of cash prizes (first prize $25; second prize $15) for the best essay on HOW TO GROW ONIONS, brought forth much interesting competition. There were received a number of good essays, evidently written by growers of experience, but of all these the best two are published in this volume. After repeated readings, we were still undecided to whom belonged the first prize. Finally, we surmounted the difficulty by omitting the second prize altogether, and awarding first prizes (each of like amount, $25) to both COL. C. H. ARLIE, of Lakeview, Oregon, and MR. T. GREINER, of Monmouth County, New Jersey. We feel quite sure that the reader will agree with us in this decision. Both writers have handled the subject very ably, and fortunately each enters more into detail where the other writes more in general. Both writers are men of extended experience as Onion Growers, and the two essays give all needed information upon the successful growing of this most important crop.

EDITOR'S PREFACE.

We have appended an article on the growing of sets, and also detailed descriptions, with illustrations of the varieties of American and Italian Onions.

Mr. Greiner, at present Editor of *The Orchard and Garden*, was known for many years as a large grower of Onions in the State of New York, and his essay will be highly valued by our readers. And yet were it not for Col. Arlie writing from the Northwest, our Western readers would miss much needed advice, while growers in the East and South can also profit by the record of his experience. Col. Arlie's chapter upon irrigation will be found particularly instructive.

W. Atlee Burpee.

Philadelphia, December 1st, 1887.

ONIONS

AND

HOW TO GROW THEM.

WITH NOTES ON VARIETIES.

BY T. GREINER, MONMOUTH CO., N. J.

With perhaps the only exceptions of celery and asparagus, there is no crop of the farm garden more exacting in its requirements as to food and attendance, or more remunerative when well managed, than that of onions from seed. The territory where this vegetable can be grown successfully extends almost over every State in the Union, and in all localities where the crop meets with ready sale at prices approaching or exceeding $1.00 per bushel it offers to the skilled grower one of the best chances to get a relatively large amount of money from a small piece of land. On the other hand, when mismanaged, it leaves a chance for considerable loss. A *large* crop must

9

be the grower's aim, as *average* crops hardly ever leave much margin of profit. The efforts should not be spread over so large an area that the available working forces might at any time be unequal to the task of doing all the work thoroughly and just at the time when needed. This is the point where the novice often makes a mistake, the sure consequence of which is partial or entire failure and disgust with the business.

Six hundred bushels to the acre is not an unusually large crop; eight hundred bushels and upward are frequently grown by good market gardeners, and I could tell a still bigger story from my own experience.

SOIL.

A satisfactory crop can be grown on almost any soil, provided it be well filled with vegetable matter (humus), well fertilized, and thoroughly drained. These requisites are indispensable. For the North, however, I would prefer soil in which sand predominates; for the South the heavier, cooler soil of the river bottoms. Well-drained, well-subdued muck lands generally offer every condition of full success everywhere. To avoid an unnecessary increase of the already large amount of labor which the crop requires, the soil should be free from stones, coarse gravel, rubbish, and especially from foul weeds and weed seeds. There is nothing to hinder planting the same piece to onions for many years in succession.

MANURE.

Eighty two-horse loads of the best compost per acre is not an excessive quantity. Very rich garden soils, however, which have been heavily manured year after year for some time previously, will produce one or two large crops with no other fertilizer except nitrate of soda, applied in two or three rations, at the rate of from 600 to 750 pounds per acre in the aggregate. Most muck lands can dispense with stable manure, and will raise a respectable crop with none but "commercial fertilizers." On such soils a good superphosphate may be applied at the rate of 1500 or more pounds per acre, but it is always advisable to supplement it with potash, best in the form of unleached wood ashes. If such are used freely, say at the rate of 100 bushels or more per acre, a smaller quantity of superphosphate than without it may be sufficient. The special "onion manures" advertised by many of our fertilizer manufacturers contain all the elements of plant food, and can be used freely and with entire confidence. Near the sea coast onion growers find one of the best of available manures in seaweed composted with stable manure. Horse manure from city stables, which is almost free from litter, generally gives good results, and so does hen manure, especially when composted and applied as a top dressing. For obvious reasons, all manure used on the onion field should be entirely free from weed seeds. Manure which is in the least coarse must be plowed in. If well decomposed and broken up fine, I would prefer to have it thoroughly mixed with the surface soil, by means of cultivator or harrow, or both.

When the bulbs are about half grown the plant food in the soil generally becomes partly exhausted. A top dressing of ashes, phosphate or other manure at this time will help to bring the crop to perfection, and should not be neglected.

PREPARATION OF THE SOIL.

A crop of carrots, parsnips or other close-planted vegetable fits the ground admirably for a succeeding crop of onions. Any farmer who knows how to prepare a field for wheat in the most thorough manner will find no difficulty in preparing an onion-seed bed properly. The ground had best be plowed in the fall, and thus exposed to the winter's frosts. At the very earliest date in spring that the land will bear working (March being preferable to April, and April to May, even in the colder portions of the United States) spread the compost thickly over the field, and at once either plow again, or (what is generally the better plan) mix it thoroughly with the surface soil by means of a suitable cultivator. Then apply a top dressing of hen manure, wood ashes, superphosphate, muriate of potash or whatever there is at hand for the purpose, harrow thoroughly, roll and harrow again, repeating, if necessary, until the soil presents a perfectly smooth and even surface, free from lumps. In some cases, especially when the soil is stony or encumbered with rubbish, it may be advisable to apply the "finishing touch" with a garden rake, leaving stones and rubbish in straight windrows running in the same direction intended for the onion rows. On most soils, however, this inconvenient job can easily be avoided.

SEED.

With onions, more than with any other vegetable, cauliflower only excepted, the outcome depends largely on the seed. *Good* seed alone can bring a glad harvest. Onion seed should be strictly fresh, for its germinating powers are greatly weakened (if not lost) and always unreliable the second season.* It should be obtained from a reliable grower or dealer, for there is always a large stock of poor, worse than worthless, seed in the market. Cheapness in onion seed carries with it a suspicion of inferiority. The grower can ill afford to run risks for the sake of

---

* We have found, by repeated tests, that first-class samples of onion seed, carefully stored in our warehouse, germinate well the second season and frequently retain their vitality perfectly. All the seed should be purchased, however, long enough in advance to permit a personal test by the grower, whether there is doubt in the mind of the purchaser or not; thus all risk as to vitality is avoided. The germinating qualities depend largely on the weight and plump body of the seed, as when there has been a poor season for perfecting the seed, we have found seed a year old to have better germinating qualities than the new crop.—ED.

saving a few dollars when he has hundreds at stake in his prospective onion crop. By all means go sure; pay a good price and plant good seed.

SOWING THE SEED.

Just as soon as the ground is in readiness, and while the surface is yet fresh and moist, the seed should be sown. This, though quite a simple operation, requires care. The leading implements used for the purpose are Matthews' Garden Drill and Planet Jr. Seed Sower.* With one of these, one man can sow an acre of onions per day with the greatest ease. It is only necessary to set the drill properly for the kind of seed to be sown, and to learn how to manage it, paying attention that the seed continues to run freely. Sometimes the hopper becomes clogged, or the seed tube filled up with soil or rubbish, and if not noticed and remedied, whole rows may be skipped in sowing, to the great annoyance and loss of the grower.

I myself, and perhaps every expert gardener, can sow seed by hand in light furrows made with a hand marker just as regularly as can be done by means of the drill, which latter, however, is greatly to be preferred for larger jobs.

Let the rows run the long way of the field. Mark off the first row or stretch a line. Straight-

---

*The seed drill should be a drill simply; the combined implements, with hoeing and weeding attachments, are not only more expensive, but are also much more liable to get out of order.—ED.

ness of the rows. adds to the attractiveness of the field and increases the grower's interest in his work. The rows should be close (in order to get the largest crop obtainable), yet not too close for ease and convenience in cultivation. Sixteen inches is just about right.

AMOUNT OF SEED PER ACRE.

For soils which are in a perfect state of preparation, especially if of a moist, mucky character, three pounds of water-cleaned seed are a sufficiency, but it will be safer for the novice to sow four pounds. On uplands, especially if somewhat stony, lumpy or liable to "bake," or otherwise not in first-class order, a still greater amount of seed— up to six pounds and more—should be used, in order to avoid risks. I, for my part, however, would not undertake to raise onions, were I compelled to plant on soil the condition of which makes the use of six or eight pounds of seed necessary.

ROLLING.

Running a hand garden roller over every row after sowing the seed is not strictly necessary, but advisable, especially when the soil was not in a perfect state of preparation.* It insures prompt germination in all cases.

---

* Too much stress cannot be laid upon the use of the roller in all seed sowing.—Ed.

CULTIVATION.

The fight against weeds must commence in good earnest at the very moment when the plants appear above ground, so that the rows can be seen. A good wheel hoe or hand cultivator is indispensable in the onion field. I prefer Ruhlman's Wheel Hoe or Gregory's Finger Weeder; but Matthews' Improved Hand Cultivator, Planet Jr. Hand Hoe or the Gem Hand Wheel Hoe are all good tools, and either of them will answer the purpose. It is generally advisable to go twice in a row at each cultivation, once close to the plants at the right, the second time close to the plants at the left. This disposes of all the weeds just sprouting between the rows and loosens the surface. The operation may be repeated once a week all through the season, to advantage; and it *must* be done at least often enough to *prevent* all weed growth.

It is to be deplored that the large majority of our market gardeners as yet stubbornly refuse to substitute the modern wheel hoe for the old-fashioned hand hoe, and thus carelessly throw aside the much-needed opportunity of reducing their labor account one-half. The possession of one or more of the modern "weed slayers" puts in our hands the power to banish the weeds from our gardens and truck patches almost entirely, and at an inconsiderable cost compared with what it used to be.*

---

* This should have the strongest commendation; these implements not only kill the weeds, but work the soil into a fine, loose tilth, and, by

HAND WEEDING.

The cultivator has left the rows of plants them-selves untouched, and they now appear as strips from one to two inches in width. Weed growth on these must be prevented, requiring often considerable work on hands and knees. Drawing a steel rake across the row is a satisfactory way of breaking the crust and disturbing the weeds just sprouting, for *some* soils, but not practicable on all. Considerable hand weeding is required in every onion field.

I have sometimes employed young boys to do the weeding; but it is only in rare cases that we meet with a bright youngster who does the work well and expeditiously. Such a one is a treasure, and should properly be humored, while all other chaps who slight their job should not be allowed to remain in the patch. It does not pay cost to hire unintelligent labor. Good, willing work-men, who receive fair wages, do the work as cheaply and *very much better* than the average heed-less youngsters.

Each man is to be provided with a good hand weeder, such as *Laing's* or *Haseltine's*, or with a gardener's trowel or common iron spoon. Down goes the whole working force on hands and knees, each man a-straddle of one row, but skipping every other row for the sake of allowing plenty of room

---

the admission of air to the roots and undersoil, double the value of the manure.—ED.

2

to work. The soil is now carefully scraped away from the plants at each side, and remaining weeds must be removed with the fingers or the edge or corner of the implement in use. When done, the row is entirely free from every vestige of weed, and the crust thoroughly broken up.* On the " return trips " the skipped rows receive the same treatment. The hand weeding will have to be repeated at least once, oftener twice, and in some cases even more times ; certainly, however, as often as weeds appear among the onions.

INJURIOUS INSECTS.

The onion maggot (larva of onion fly) does much damage to the onion crop in some localities. In May or June the fly deposits its eggs on the leaves near the surface of the ground. The maggots soon hatch and descend to the base of the

---

* We would suggest that the amount of hand weeding may be lessened by each skilled hand being supplied with a good steel hoe, the blade of which is *not more than 1½ inches broad and sharpened on the grindstone twice a day when in use*, with which to run over the row both in weeding and in thinning. The belt of two or three inches left by the cultivator can thus be reduced to the actual span taken up by the young plants. The thinning process can also be successfully done by this narrow implement ; thus, while not superseding altogether the hand weeding it does away with at least three-quarters of the " hands and knees " work. Of course this can only be accomplished by the skilled and careful laborer. We would also recommend, where the rows are far enough apart, Lee's Horse Hoe, designed and patented by a Philadelphia market gardener for cultivating onions ; it has broad hoes, which are turned at the sides, and which, by a steady hand, can be worked within one inch of the row without throwing dirt upon the row of young seedlings.—ED.

young bulb, where they feed for about two weeks. The attacked onions turn yellow, and should be carefully lifted out of the ground, maggots and all, and destroyed. This will head off the second brood. The application of air-slacked lime close to the plants is recommended as a reasonably sure remedy. So is that of fresh gas lime.

THINNING.

Onions stand crowding pretty well; but overcrowding must result in uneven and inferior size of the bulbs. At the second weeding the plants had best be thinned to stand about two inches apart in the row, leaving the strongest plants and removing the weaker ones.

HARVESTING THE CROP.

In July or August, when the tops have died down, the crop is ready for harvesting. The bulbs can be pulled up by hand, leaving them in windrows to cure. The same object can often be accomplished much easier and quicker by drawing a wooden rake across the rows, leaving the product of three or four rows in a windrow, as mentioned. The work of " pulling " requires little skill, and youngsters may be employed to good advantage.

When thus left in windrows for a few days, the tops dry and generally waste away. The bulbs are then picked and sorted over, the remnants of tops twisted or cut off, and the crop sold right out of the field or stored under shelter.

MARKETING.

Careful sorting and grading is of much less importance in the local markets than in the large city market. I have had occasion to watch the commission stands in the cities, and to observe that the barrel containing bulbs all of an even size (which makes the lot attractive) will sell more readily and always at a higher figure than the barrel holding a mixture of all sizes. Carefully grading the crop before putting them in barrels for shipment, is necessary to realize the highest market price. The work of sorting and grading pays as well as any other labor in connection with the business.

WINTERING.

The best advice I could give to the novice is: Don't attempt to winter so perishable an article as onions! Considerable loss can seldom be avoided at best. Sell the crop in the fall, as early as practicable, and thus avoid much loss from shrinkage and rot. Still, there are various ways of wintering onions successfully. They can be pitted like apples, covering somewhat more lightly and leaving a chance for ventilation at the top. Or they can be spread in a dry loft, piled up a foot or more high, and at the approach of severe weather covered with straw, hay or matting. Light freezing does not hurt them, if they are allowed to thaw gradually and not handled while frozen; but if exposed to a temperature lower than 15° above zero, they are liable to rot. I have frequently wintered onions in slitted barrels and in crates and baskets in the cellar quite successfully.

WHITE GLOBE ONION.

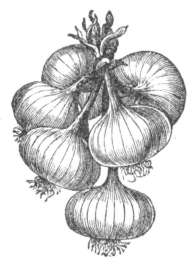

EARLY WHITE QUEEN.

·VARIETIES.

For the market gardener at the North and in many localities further South, no varieties of their respective color combine more good points than *Yellow Danvers* (with its various strains), *Red Wethersfield* and *White Globe.* All these attain large size, are very reliable for bottoming, productive and popular in the markets. *White Globe* is superlatively handsome, but ought to be cured under shelter, in order to preserve its clean, white, attractive appearance.

Other varieties popular with market gardeners are *Extra Early Red*, which is quite early, of medium size, solid and often profitable in cold, mucky soils at the North; *Large Red Globe* and

Southport Large Yellow Globe, which resemble *White Globe* in almost every feature except color; *Yellow Dutch* or *Yellow Strasburg,* a good keeper and quite prolific, but undoubtedly inferior to *Yellow Danvers;* and *White Silver Skin* or *White Portugal,* largely used for pickling and for " white sets."

Among the new Italian onions, we find many especially adapted for the South. Of them I will mention the various strains of the *Giant Rocca,* the *Giant White Tripoli* and *Red Mammoth Tripoli* or *Bermuda Red,* all of which are of very large size. The *new Mammoth Silver King* and *Mammoth Pompeii* produce the largest bulbs of all varieties now known. *New Queen,* on the other hand, is quite small, but its extreme earliness, its beauty and keeping qualities render it altogether a desirable sort for many purposes.

ONION CULTURE

BY

IRRIGATION.

BY COL. C. H. ARLIE, OF OREGON.

In treating this subject I shall relate my experience and observation, and however this may differ from the practice of others, I shall still have the assurance that the methods herein described are practical and not theoretical.

The minuteness of detail may seem to the experienced like going over common ground, but let the older heads bear in mind that the "A B C's" are difficult to the beginner; and the tyro in onion culture may easily magnify a molehill of difficulty into a mountain.

It shall be the aim of the writer to give directions sufficiently plain and full, so that a man who did not know enough about onions to tell whether he had to dig down in the ground for the seed or climb up in the tree and shake them,

23

could set about, with some degree of intelligence, to grow a crop of onions.

1. **Kinds of Soil.**
2. **Preparation of Ground.**
3. **Varieties.**
4. **Planting the Seed.**
5. **Cultivation.**
6. **Harvesting the Crop.**
7. **Storing for Winter.**
8. **The Importance of Good Seed.**
9. **General Remarks.**
10. **Irrigation.**

KINDS OF SOIL.

It is probable that the onion will succeed under a wider range of soils and conditions than is supposed by a great many. I do not lay so much stress upon the particular kind of soil as upon the preparation of the ground and the subsequent treatment of the crop.

It is the general experience of onion growers, however, that a rich, sandy loam is to be preferred. Too much sand is not desirable, from the fact that such soil would lack the requisite strength; and clay or "sticky" land is to be avoided. Onions, to do their best, require a great deal of nourishment, and they should accordingly be planted on your richest, strongest-growing soil—provided it is not naturally wet land. In the extreme West onions are grown successfully on "Sage-brush" land. Nearly all of this is of a sandy nature, not calculated to withstand drought, but producing fine crops where irrigated and properly fertilized. Land that is naturally moist, as, for instance, the edge of meadows, might grow a crop all right to start with, but the chances are that they would be late in maturing and that a large portion of them would run to "stiff-necks" or scallions. (Please pronounce this "scallions" and not "scullions," as it is frequently called.)

We will now suppose that we are about to plant a piece of ground that has never been in onions before. From the smallness of the young plants and the tediousness of cultivation it will be apparent that it is of the utmost importance to keep the ground as free from weeds as possible during the previous year. For this purpose we select an acre of land that is as nearly level as may be. In the spring we will seed it to carrots, or parsnips, or potatoes, and cultivate thoroughly enough to prevent any weeds from seeding. It is claimed by some that carrots are the best crop to precede onions; not only from their going deep into the ground and mellowing the soil, but also owing to their beneficial effect on the ensuing crop. Some recommend corn, but this leaves a large amount of rubbish to be removed in the way of roots.

When this crop is harvested in the fall, we rake up and burn or cart off all the litter that can be gathered with a garden rake. Just before freezing weather sets in, the land is plowed to a moderate depth. We now go on to it with a lute (a plank scraper, five or six feet wide, with plow handles, similar to what is used on a brickyard), and if the ground is rather uneven we take, in addition, a common two-horse road scraper. Wherever there is a bump or an elevation it is cut down and filled into the nearest hollow. After the roughest of the work is done in this manner, we lay the ground off in imaginary beds, say ten or twelve feet wide, and running lengthwise with a very slight incline. After passing over it with the lute, which acts as a leveler and clod crusher, we can detect swells and hollows that were not noticeable before. When it is thoroughly leveled, we next apply well-rotted manure, at the rate of thirty loads to the acre.* Before applying this manure, if the ground is not free from lumps it should be plowed and harrowed until well "fined." This may be horse manure or a combination of the various kinds usually found in barnyard manure, but it should be well rotted, thoroughly pulverized and free from trash and lumps that would interfere with the working of the seed drill. After spreading the manure as evenly as possible, the ground is again plowed to an ordinary depth, at the same time following in the furrow with a "subsoil" plow. This loosens up the ground to a depth of twelve inches or more without bringing the under soil to the sur-

---

* Even double this quantity of manure per acre can be profitably applied.—ED.

face—a thing which is to be avoided in onion culture. If it were in the spring, the ground would be harrowed and cross-harrowed thoroughly with an "Acme" harrow. But on fall plowing we want the ground as much as possible exposed to the action of the frost through the winter, and for this reason it is not harrowed. When spring comes, the ground is simply harrowed and worked up with a rake.

VARIETIES.

There are several varieties of onions, the three distinct types of which are red, white and yellow. Among the red varieties the two best known and most generally cultivated are the Red Wethersfield and the Extra Early Red. The Wethersfield is a large, coarse-grained onion that is extensively grown in many sections, and on congenial soil produces a heavy crop. The Extra Early Red is smaller and earlier than the Wethersfield, and a much more reliable "bottomer." It is, probably, the surest onion when the seasons are very short. There is also the Red Globe, similar to the others in color, but round in shape; not quite so large as the Wethersfield, but a fine appearing onion, and I believe a more reliable variety than the latter. These are all different types of the same onion, bred up with some particular end in view.

Of yellow varieties, the most popular are the Large Yellow Strasburg and Danvers Yellow.

(The term silverskin is in some places incorrectly applied to pale yellow varieties, and in other localities it means a pure white.) The Strasburg was formerly cultivated largely, but the Danvers has superseded it to a great extent. Most of the white varieties are of foreign introduction and are not considered so hardy and vigorous as the others. The best deserving of mention are the White Globe and Silverskin or White Portugal. The white onions when properly cured present a handsome appearance for market, but they have a delicate skin, requiring care in curing and handling, and their cultivation is confined more particularly to the Southern States and California.*

The market will determine the choice of variety to a certain extent, but it is safe to say that the great bulk of the onion crop in the United States is grown from the Danvers Yellow and the Red Wethersfield. It is claimed that in some markets the Wethersfield is preferred, but for my own part, if I had to confine myself to one variety, I should take the Yellow Danvers in preference to any other. They are a reliable onion to bottom, while the Wethersfield, on some soils, shows a strong

---

* We must differ with Col. Arlie on this point, as white onions are very successfully grown in the Middle and Eastern States. In our Philadelphia markets they sell the most readily and bring the highest prices. They are, however, very uncertain seed bearers, and the seed is always considerably higher in price than the red and yellow varieties. —ED.

EXTRA EARLY RED ONION.

tendency to scallions. The Danvers is a splendid winter keeper (given the preference by many dealers over any other); it presents a finer appearance in the sack than the Wethersfield, and in nearly all the Western markets it is quoted above the red varieties.

Of the red varieties, the Extra Early Red is generally preferred on account of its early maturity. But, whatever the variety, do not plant cheap seed. Buy the best that you can get.

PLANTING.

As soon in the spring as the ground is in working condition seeding begins. Do not be afraid of getting them in too early. For this purpose I use a " Planet Jr." drill.*

The choice of a drill is perhaps largely a matter of early training. The two most common drills in use are Matthews' and the Planet Jr., both of which are good machines. I have always used the Planet Jr., and find it satisfactory in every way. The ground should be hand-raked to make it as fine as possible, and as fast as one bed is prepared it should be seeded *before allowing time for the finely fertilized surface to dry out any.*

---

* Nearly all Eastern seedsmen keep on hand or furnish these drills. " Planet Jr." or Matthews' Combined drill cost in the East, $12.00; on the Pacific Coast, $15.00. These will sow nearly all vegetable seeds that can be drilled. For onion culture on a large scale there are drills made expressly for onion seed; dropping and covering two rows at a time. Such, for instance, as " Holbrook's" or " Hill & Jennings'."

Set your drill to cover the seed three-fourths of an inch deep.* Some will tell you to cover one-fourth of an inch deep, but when they talk that way to you heed them not. I shall hereafter put mine in one inch. Put the rows fourteen inches apart and be careful to get the first row straight, because all the others will be gauged by it. But whether straight or crooked, be careful to maintain the same distance between the rows all the time. The necessity for this is apparent when you come to

* It should be borne in mind that the practice of growers in different sections varies widely. To illustrate: Mr. W. H. White, of Westborough, Mass., says: "If the seed is in every respect good, three pounds are sufficient for an acre;" while Mr. W. H. Ball, of Springfield, Mo., says: "I drill the seed in one foot apart, using six pounds of seed to the acre," and then adds: "We never thin onions."

And one grower wants them in one-fourth inch deep, while another insists on putting them down one inch. One reason why many growers sow them so shallow, perhaps, comes from the old practice of sowing broadcast, like ruta bagas. Then, again, some claim that, in order to bottom well, the bulb of the onion should be entirely above ground, like a turnip.

I am not sure of this. People in the West, where irrigation is practiced, get a great many ideas from experience that were not dreamed of in the East. For instance, it might surprise some Eastern gardeners to see corn and peas plowed in to a depth of six inches; and I have seen onion seed put into a furrow that had been made by a plow to the wheel hoe (and even with a "single-shovel" plow), and then covered with a hand hoe. It would seem that the seed in this case must have been down at least two and possibly three inches.

A drying wind for a short time, or a few days of hot weather, will easily absorb the moisture to a depth of one-fourth inch, and if the seed are only down that deep, a great many are liable to perish for want of moisture just as they sprout. Whereas, if they had been down an inch they could get well rooted before the ground dried to that depth. I am done with this "surface" planting.—AUTHOR.

cultivate; because your wheel hoe is set to cut a certain width, and if the rows crowd together in places, the hoe will cut out the plants wherever the space narrows down. The roller will probably press the earth down sufficiently without any further work. I am aware that some writers lay great stress upon "firming the soil;" and it is doubtless a good plan where the ground is dry, but judgment must be used, as, if there is much moisture in the ground, there is a liability of packing it too much. *

In one season I put in a crop on the 17th of April. The ground, after having been hand-raked, had laid a week, so that the moisture seemed to be all out of it. In addition to this, the roller attachment to the drill was missing, so that the soil that covered the seed was sifted on to it in the loosest possible manner. Expecting to have to irrigate in order to sprout the seed, I did not firm the soil in the least. Shortly after the seeding was finished, the ground was covered with a coat of snow, and in fourteen days from time of planting, some of the seed began to break through. Rolling could not have brought the seed any quicker. Of course, if the snow had

---

* Would it not be very injudicious to sow seed when the ground is too wet and sticky to *roll?* The drill would not work well in such soil; wherever the sower stepped it would become packed and hard, as much as if passed over by the roller. The rolling packs the soil firmly around the seed on all sides; if left to lie in a hollow space, the seed would be apt to become too wet and rot off.—ED.

not fallen, the seed would not have sprouted. But without any moisture in the ground, rolling could not have sprouted them.* Then, again, one spring I had put in some seed for sets, and thinking to retain the moisture in the soil I hoed the rows while the ground was wet. This, of course, was wrong, and packed the ground so that not more than one-third of the seed came.

CULTIVATION.

About fifteen or twenty days after seeding, the plants will begin to show themselves, and just as soon as you can trace the rows distinctly, go into them with the wheel hoes. For this purpose I use "Planet Jr." double-wheel hoe and "Ruhlman's" single-wheel hoe. The single-wheel hoe runs between the rows, while the double-wheel straddles them and cuts on both sides. For the special purpose for which "Ruhlman's" hoe is intended, it is superior to the "Planet Jr.," but for the first cultivation and while the plants are small I prefer the "Planet Jr." The hoe blades can be adjusted so as to throw the earth slightly away from the plants, and thus admit of very early and close cultivation. Some go through

---

* We must differ with Col. Arlie here, as in a dry season, "firming the soil" certainly increases the chances of the seed germinating successfully. Did not the weight of snow serve to *lightly firm* the soil? Of course, sowing so wet, if the ground had been gone over with a heavy roller, it would have become solid and hard. But is it judicious to plant in such wet ground, though this was an accidental success?—ED.

3

the onions the first time with a scuffle hoe, but I
see no necessity for this, inasmuch as the wheel
hoe can be used without covering or disturbing the
young plants.   But, whatever you use, go at it just
as soon as the weeds can be seen.   Don't wait for
the seeds to start.   No matter how brave you feel,
it is not policy to give weeds any advantage.   And
whenever you let them get their heads above
ground, they are gaining just so much advantage
over the misguided agriculturist and the latest
improved machinery.

If there is danger of the weeds starting before
the onions come through, you can mix about one-
tenth turnip or radish seed with the onions at
time of sowing.   As these germinate so much
sooner, it will enable you to trace the rows before
the onions can be seen. If radish seeds are
used, be careful to see that they are smaller in
size than the onion, so as not to clog the drill.*

For the first two months the onions should be
cultivated every ten days. When about four
inches high thin them to two inches in the row.†

---

* Where no leveling attachment is used, or even where it is, it is
frequently possible to go between the rows with the wheel hoe before
the seeds germinate, as the soil between the rows is not disturbed by
the drill, and the weed seeds germinate more quickly than where it has
been stirred by the drill. Of course, there is no occasion for this where
the soil is as free from weed seeds as it should be, nor where the
ground has all been freshly worked immediately before sowing. The
sowing of the other seeds is quite an original suggestion, but would
make trouble if not immediately thinned out.—ED.

† I believe it is not the general custom in the East to thin onions.

At the same time go through them on your hands and knees with a hand weeder and remove all the weeds in the row that the wheel hoe cannot reach. For the purpose of thinning, we use an onion hoe (a long narrow blade with the socket in the center and a cutting surface on each end. One end cuts about two and one-half inches; the reverse end about one and one-half); walking sidewise, we cut out with the narrow blade of the hoe most of the plants necessary to be gotten rid of. Then, when we go through on our hands and knees to weed them, we thin out the remainder by hand, using for this purpose " Noye's Hand Weeder"* (a small diamond-shaped instrument, costing thirty cents). The plants should not be allowed to get too large before thinning, as it will disturb their roots.

But I do not see how the most desirable results can be attained without thinning. We know that if onions are planted thickly enough their growth will be checked so as to form sets instead of large onions. Experience proves that two plants cannot be grown on a space just sufficient to grow one comfortably, without dwarfing the size of each. Then having ascertained what space is necessary, it is our business to give each plant room enough to develop itself. Now the first thing to be desired by the onion grower is a good stand. If, then, we want the plants to stand two inches apart, it is evident that we cannot do it by planting the seed that distance. We have to provide against every contingency of weather, worms, and defective seed, and our only safeguard is to sow thickly and then thin down to the required distance. Is this not as true of the onion as of the watermelon or turnip?—AUTHOR.

*We would recommend, as better suited to the purpose, the *Excelsior Hand Weeder*, which has five teeth, making a claw in shape of the fingers of the hand. It leaves the dirt finer and looser than the cutting edge of the Noye's Weeder, and the cost is no greater.—ED.

They will probably require four hand weedings, and the cultivation will extend over a period of about three months, or as long as the weeds continue to grow. Some do not like to work among the onions after they begin to bottom, claiming that it has a tendency to make them " blast." But it is frequently necessary to remove weeds some time after they have commenced to bottom. When the tops of the first onions fall over, then nothing more is done with them until they are ready to harvest.

HARVESTING.

When the tops have turned yellow and all dried up next to the bulb, the onion is ripe. As some time elapses between the falling of the top and the complete ripening of the bulb, and as a portion of the crop will be much later than the first, we let them stand until about time for frost.* The practice of rolling onions is followed by some, thinking it necessary to ripen the crop (i. e., rolling a barrel over the rows after they have commenced to fall down). If the right kind of seed is sown and the crop has proper attention, the onions are going to ripen when the time comes, just as surely as a melon or a potato. And if the seed is only fit to grow scallions, why scallions they will be. I have just about as much faith in

---

*We would caution the reader against allowing the onions to lie on the ground after the tops are well dried, as, if a rain comes, they are apt to root again. The tops also would be apt to rot and the onions become musty.—ED.

rolling onions as I have in planting them in the "right moon." But it is possible that, when a crop has been put in so late that they have not time to mature, rolling might hasten their ripening. Just to what extent, I am not prepared to say.* When the crop has ripened sufficiently, the onions are pulled, after first loosening under the row with a prong hoe or spading fork; they are then thrown into windrows, consisting of three rows of onions, where they lay for one week. Then they are piled into rounding heaps of six to ten bushels and allowed to sweat for ten days. If thoroughly dried they are now ready for storage, and they can be put into winter quarters immediately, or, by covering with six or eight inches of straw to exclude the heat of the sun and prevent the repeated freezing and thawing, they can lay here until danger of freezing weather.

STORING FOR WINTER.

An ordinary cellar is a poor place in which to keep onions, from the fact that it is too moist and too warm. If it were perfectly dry, and the temperature could be kept at about 35°, it would answer finely. An onion will stand any degree of cold, but will not stand repeated freezing and

---

* The idea in rolling is to bend over and partly break off the tops, so as to check the flow of nutrition from the roots into the tops, and confine it to increasing the size and quick ripening of the bulb.—Ed.

thawing. If they are to be frozen at all, they must be kept that way until spring. And if not allowed to freeze, they should be kept just as near the freezing point as may be, in order to prevent their sprouting. And they must have ventilation.

For ordinary purposes, a dry out-building with perfect ventilation is the most convenient for storage in large quantities.

Leave the tops on and take them in from the field in the afternoon when they are perfectly dry.*

The building in which they are to be stored should be so arranged that it has a free circulation of air underneath the floor. Arrange bins in the building from four to six feet in width and one foot deep, leaving a space of a foot or so next the outer wall. The first bin should be raised six inches from the floor, and the bottom of the bin should be composed of three-inch slats, having a two-inch space between each one. Now place good dry straw in the bottom of the bin, sufficient to make two inches when weighted down, and fill in with onions until nearly level with the top. Cover with straw, sufficient to exclude all light from the onions. Continue next layer of bins on top of this in same manner, leaving sufficient space between each layer of bins to admit a free

---

*The Colonel gives no special reason for leaving the tops on. It would take up extra room, would make dirt, and is against all canons of good and neat gardening.—ED.

circulation of air. Have windows so constructed
that the sun cannot shine into the room at any
time. After good freezing weather has fairly set
in, select some night when it is cold enough to
freeze the onion solid and throw open the doors
and windows. After this the temperature in the
room should be kept below 32°, and only venti-
late it when the temperature is lower than in the
building.* In this manner the onions may be
kept until warm weather. Let them thaw out
with the covering on and do not handle them
until all frost is out of them.

THE IMPORTANCE OF GOOD SEED.

The value attached to good onion seed by old
growers may be a source of wonder to the inex-
perienced, and it is oftentimes entirely overlooked
by the beginner in the business. Let me try to
explain why cheap onion seed is not cheap. The
onion stalk attains a height of, say, from sixteen
to twenty inches when fully matured. As the
onion develops and begins to ripen, the stalk falls
over and shrivels up at the bulb. This forms
a ripe onion. But a certain percentage of the
onions, although attaining fair size, will remain
large and stiff around the neck, constituting a
" stiff neck " or scallion. The scallion, although
good to eat, will not keep through the winter, and

---

* This would require keeping them till spring (until the frost is all
out of them), when they would have to be marketed very quickly,
though no doubt they would bring a higher price.—ED.

is, consequently, not marketable like a matured onion. Now, the onion, of all vegetables, is perhaps the most susceptible of being bred up to a high degree. If we should select the seed of scallions for a few years, we would soon get something that would grow scallions almost to a certainty. On the other hand, if we select one of the earliest and best shaped onions, with a very small neck (when green), to propagate our seed from, and continue this selection for years, we will have a strain of seed in which the scallion is almost eradicated. Inasmuch as every scallion is like so much dead stock on the market, it is evident that the smaller the percentage of scallions the more valuable the seed to the grower. It is exactly this feature that makes the seed of the conscientious careful seedsman valuable; while the unscrupulous onion grower may sell all his marketable onions, set out his scallions next spring, and in the fall have a fine lot of cheap seed for sale.

GENERAL REMARKS.

In raising onions for market where the growing season is short, your first consideration will be the selection of a variety that will be certain to make itself during the season. The matter of next importance is the particular variety that is in greatest demand in your market. If the onion crop is short and prices high, anything will sell; but if the market is glutted, you will find dealers very particular. One grower may be able to work off his entire crop because he has the right variety, while his neighbor is unable to dispose of his for just the opposite reason.

In selecting a seed drill and wheel hoe, let me strongly urge the advantage of a separate drill and cultivator, instead of buying the combined machine. Combined machines of any kind are not as good as separate ones, and the difference in cost is not enough to compensate for the extra convenience and thorough work.

There are onion pests in some localities that work on the crop more or less, while in other localities they are practically exempt from such ravages. The onion maggot is very destructive in some places, and occasionally the "wire worm" does considerable damage. The wire worm does its work while the plants are small, and if they stand thickly enough the loss may not amount to much.

I know of no remedy that is practical on a large scale for any of these pests.

IRRIGATION.

In irrigating, there are two methods of applying the water, which, as regards theory and practice, are entirely distinct. One is called flooding, and the other furrow irrigation. Flooding, as the name implies, means the complete covering of the ground by having the beds banked up so as to confine the water. Furrow irrigation consists in running the water in a small trench between each row of plants. For flooding, the ground may be laid off in beds from ten to fifteen or even twenty feet in width, and about ten rods long. The size of the beds will be governed, somewhat, by the water supply. A big head of water can be got over much wider beds to advantage than a small stream.

The beds, sidewise, should be perfectly level; and it is better to have them level lengthwise as well, though they may have a slight incline. If the beds are level lengthwise the ground can be wet to any desired depth. Water may be turned on until it stands one inch in depth all over the bed —which would be equivalent to a rainfall of perhaps one and a half or two inches—or it may be turned on to a depth of six inches, according to the requirements of the case. If the bed has an incline, the lower end should be left open, allowing the water to pass off, else that end will receive a great deal more water and the ground will probably become packed.

The soil, of course, should have moisture enough in it at the time of planting to germinate the seed. This the operator can regulate by late fall irrigating (before plowing).

If the ground contains an abundance of moisture when the seed is sown, it may not be necessary to irrigate for a month after the plants are up; but the proper time to apply the water must be determined by each individual case. The first application of water in the spring should be as light as may be, from the fact that the soil at that time is very loose and absorbs water much more rapidly than later in the season. As soon after irrigating as the ground begins to dry (perhaps forty-eight hours, more or less), and before it has had time to bake, it is run over with the wheel hoe, just skimming the surface. Then it is followed with the cultivator teeth. It then lies in this condition until dry enough to require another irrigating; and so on through the season. This leaves the ground loose and mellow after each irrigating and thoroughly exposed to the chemical action of the atmosphere. It is this repeated mellowing and stirring of the soil that constitutes the charm and effectiveness of irrigation. The cultivator is not dependent upon the uncertainties of rain, and intelligent labor receives its fullest measure of compensation.

During the heat of the season the crop will need irrigating once a week and sometimes twice (depending a great deal upon the character of the soil). Toward the latter part of the season it will not be so particular about stirring the soil after each irrigating. When the first onions begin to fall down irrigating stops.

For furrow irrigation, the onions are planted on level ground (just the same as where irrigation is not practiced). The rows should be laid out so as to have a fall of from six inches to a foot in every ten rods. Where the ground is quite sloping, the first row may be laid out with a triangle (a wooden frame in the shape of a letter A, measuring twelve feet from base to base and having a plumb-bob in the center), with a fall of one half-inch to every twelve feet. Then every other row can be run by this. If the fall is less than six inches to ten rods the water will be too slow in getting through; on the other hand, if the fall much exceeds twelve inches the soil will wash away. This season I had in a few rows where the fall was about three feet to ten rods; but it was altogether too much.

Now for the mode of applying the water. The rows should be about fourteen inches apart. Run the " Planet Jr." cultivator between each row, and the peculiar shape of the three teeth will leave a small furrow, at the same time not throwing enough dirt on either side to interfere with the plants. Let each one of these furrows run a very small stream of water, just sufficient to keep running but not large enough to overflow its banks. This water passes off and must have an outlet, and is allowed to run in the furrows until it has soaked the ground to the center of the rows (perhaps six hours, more or less). After the ground has sufficiently dried it is cultivated in the same manner as described in "flooding." These furrows between the rows can be made with the wheel plow, or by running the cultivator with the three teeth, or they can also be made by walking backward and dragging a common hoe with one point digging the ground in a V shape. As to which system is the better, I think it is partly a matter of taste or early education.

In Southern Colorado the flooding system is practiced exclusively. I believe the same is also true of the Mexicans through New Mexico, Arizona, and the Southwest, who have been practicing irrigation for generations. In this immediate vicinity furrow irrigation is generally followed.

Some prefer the furrow system, claiming that it does not bake and pack so badly as by flooding. But ground that is sandy enough for onions will stand flooding if properly handled. Of course, it will not do to flood the ground and then allow it to dry and bake without stirring the soil.

Theoretically, the furrow system may be better, but for my own part I like flooding. It is quick work and more evenly regulated. You can turn on what water you choose, cut it off, and pass on to the next bed. There is no waste of water, there is no fertility washed away, and I believe the soil retains the moisture better. In flooding there is the disadvantage of having the space between each bed waste ground and constantly growing a crop of weeds. In furrow irrigation there is the advantage of using every foot of ground and of being able to put in the crop without leveling up the ground so much; while there is the disadvantage of having so much water run to waste, and a portion of the applied fertility washed away. A trial of each system on a small scale will best enable each grower to decide which is best for his individual use.*

This article has been prepared at odd intervals and during evenings after a hard day's work, and in summing up its faults and shortcomings it is hoped that those who are disposed to be critical will take into consideration the circumstances under which it was composed.

---

* We think the Colonel makes decidedly a good case for the flooding system of irrigation as advantageous over the furrow system, especially on the point of utilizing all the *land, water and fertilizer.* In the furrow system a large portion of the water runs off, and must, consequently, take some of the best soil in solution, besides the danger of washing gullies.—ED.

VARIETIES OF ONIONS.

BY W. ATLEE BURPEE.

As this treatise is intended to be complete without requiring the novice to refer to seed catalogues for lists of varieties, we supplement the essays with descriptions and illustrations of the leading varieties of Onions now grown in America. These are divided into two classes: American Onions and Italian Onions. As the former are the main reliance of the grower for market, we will first describe the varieties of the

AMERICAN ONIONS.

ROUND YELLOW DANVERS.

Reliability for bottoming and large yield are both combined in this popular variety. It is extensively grown for market, and frequently produces six hundred bushels per acre from seed sown in the spring. It is a very handsome, round onion, of good size, with thin, yellow skin; flesh white, fine-grained, firm, mild and of excellent quality. It ripens early, keeps well, and sells readily. This variety is also largely used for growing sets.

YELLOW GLOBE DANVERS ONION.

LARGE RED WETHERSFIELD ONION.

YELLOW GLOBE DANVERS.

Is a selected strain of the preceding, although not really a distinct variety. The bulbs are thicker through, but not perfectly globe-shaped, like the Southport Yellow Globe, which is a later onion to mature. Altogether, a good strain of seed of this variety is probably the best for general cultivation either for market or the home garden—provided only one sort is grown. It is a splendid keeper. In England a very similar strain is known as *James' Keeping Onion.*

YELLOW STRASBURG, OR DUTCH.

One of the oldest varieties; bulbs quite flat, of good size; skin yellow; flesh white; of mild flavor; keeps well. This is the variety that formerly was used very extensively for growing Philadelphia Yellow Onion sets, and while still good for that purpose, it has of late years been nearly superseded by the Yellow Danvers. The skin is rather darker in color than the Danvers.

SOUTHPORT LARGE YELLOW GLOBE.

This is a very handsome onion, quite popular in the New England States. It is of large size and perfectly globe-shaped; skin yellow, flesh white and reasonably fine grained.

LARGE RED WETHERSFIELD.

This rivals the Yellow Danvers in its great popularity, being a standard market variety in the Eastern and Middle States. The onions are

4

SOUTHPORT YELLOW GLOBE ONION.

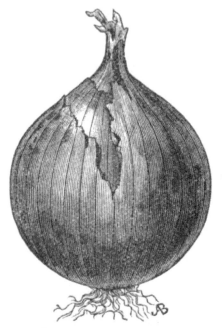

LARGE RED GLOBE ONION.

of large size, round form, somewhat flattened, but thick through. Skin deep purplish red; flesh purplish white, moderately fine grained and of rather stronger flavor than the yellow onions. If planted on unsuitable soils it is more inclined to form thick necks than the Danvers, but when well grown is a very handsome, salable onion.

EXTRA EARLY RED.

Of flattened form, not so thick through as the Wethersfield, this variety matures earlier and will often form bulbs in cold and mucky soils where other varieties fail. It is highly esteemed in the Northwest.

LARGE RED GLOBE.

As shown in the illustration, this is a very handsome variety, and is deserving of general cultivation. It matures quite early (none of the perfectly globe-shaped onions are as early as the flat varieties), grows to a large size; skin deep red; flesh fine-grained, mild and tender.

LARGE WHITE GLOBE, OR SOUTHPORT WHITE GLOBE ONION.

Of perfect globe shape; both skin and flesh are pure white; fine-grained, of mild flavor. This is an extremely handsome onion, and commands the highest market price, but requires more careful handling than the red and yellow onions.

WHITE SILVER SKIN, OR WHITE PORTUGAL.

Very desirable for family use; flavor mild and pleasant; skin silvery white; of handsome appearance; highly esteemed for pickling when young, also for market in early winter. This is the variety of which White Onion Sets are grown, and is known in New England as *Philadelphia White*.

HARD, ROUND, SILVER SKIN.

Produces uniformly small, round and handsome onions, with an opaque, white skin that does not turn green by exposure to the sun. The onions are very compact and hard, but at the same time crisp and brittle; altogether the best pickling onion. Although of foreign origin, this can be classed as an American Onion, and has lately become in large demand by pickling establishments.

ITALIAN ONIONS.

Unlike most foreign varieties of onions, these Italian varieties bulb well in nearly all sections of the United States. While it is better for the novice in onion-growing for market to confine himself to the American varieties, he should experiment with these, and every family garden should be enriched by a few varieties of these handsome onions. As a rule, they do not keep well, but for summer and fall use are very desirable.

For some years past large quantities of Italian onions have been raised from imported seed by truckers in the South. The onions command large prices in the Philadelphia and New York markets, where they sell as Bermuda and Spanish onions.

WHITE SILVER SKIN, OR WHITE PORTUGAL.

HARD, ROUND, SILVER SKIN ONION.

The Italian onions grow rapidly, and, except the Small Queen, form fine, large bulbs, weighing from one to one and a half pounds each, the first year from seed, while several of the varieties even exceed these weights. They are all much milder in flavor than our American onions.

EARLIEST WHITE QUEEN.

The bulbs are small, flat, pure white, and of excellent flavor, but the principal recommendation is the marvelous rapidity of its growth. Sown in February, they will produce onions one or two inches in diameter early in summer. Sown in July, they will be ready to pull late in autumn, and *will keep sound for many months*, retaining their *most* exquisite flavor. One of the very best onions for pickling, making fine, hard, brittle pickles, of attractive appearance.

GOLDEN QUEEN OR GOLDEN GEM.

This is identically the same as White Queen, except in color of skin.

SILVER WHITE ETNA, OR EXTRA EARLY PEARL.

A very fine variety that grows quickly to a good marketable size; very popular, particularly in the South. The bulbs are round, flattened, with a delicate, pure white skin; flesh very mild and pleasant in flavor. It is claimed to excel most other onions of Italian origin in keeping qualities.

GOLDEN QUEEN ONION.

GIANT WHITE ROCCA, OR SILVER BALL ONION.

PALE RED ETNA, OR RED PEARL.

This differs from the preceding chiefly in color of the skin, which is a light red.

NEAPOLITAN MARZAJOLE.

A large, beautiful, silvery-white-skinned variety, of handsome, flat shape, and of very fine quality. Sown in February or March, it will produce a splendid crop early in the season. Seed sown in July will mature a crop the same season.

SILVER WHITE ETNA ONION.

GIANT ROCCA, OF NAPLES.

Of very mild, delicate flavor, immense size, handsome, globular shape, and light, reddish-brown skin. It is an excellent keeping onion, valuable alike for autumn and spring sowing. In this immediate vicinity Giant Rocca onions have been grown to weigh 1½ to 1¾ *pounds each, from seed sown in the spring.* However, if the largest possible size is desired, the smallest bulbs should be set out in the spring of the

GIANT ROCCA ONION.

second season, when they will continue to increase in size, instead of producing seed, as is the case with American onions.

GIANT WHITE ITALIAN TRIPOLI ONION.

MAMMOTH POMPEII ONION.

GIANT RED ROCCA.

This is very similar to the above, but has been selected with a view to a deeper red color of the skin.

GIANT YELLOW ROCCA, OR GOLDEN GLOBE TRIPOLI.

A very handsome onion, of immense size, with light yellow skin.

GIANT WHITE ROCCA, OR SILVER BALL.

This might be described as a *mammoth* White Globe Onion, although the bulbs are not so uniform in shape as our American White Globe.

GIANT WHITE ITALIAN TRIPOLI.

A very large, round, flat, white onion, sometimes called *El Paso*, or *Large Mexican*. It readily grows to weigh 1½ pounds from the black seed the first season.

RED MAMMOTH TRIPOLI, OR BERMUDA RED.

Similar in shape and size to the Giant White Tripoli. Skin thin and of a rich blood-red color; flesh white, fine-grained, mild and pleasant; of large growth.

BURPEE'S MAMMOTH SILVER KING.

The Mammoth Silver King Onion, named and introduced by us in 1884, grows to a most remarkable size—*larger than any other variety in cultivation*, excepting only the New Mammoth Pompeii. The bulbs are of attractive form, flattened, but thick through. The average diameter of the onions is

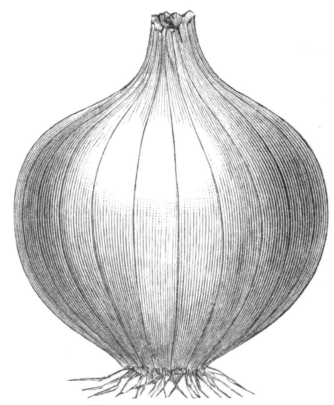

GIANT YELLOW ROCCA ONION.

RED MAMMOTH TRIPOLI ONION.

from 5 to 7½ inches—thus making the circumference from 15 to 22 inches. Single bulbs often attain weights of from 2½ to 4 pounds each, *the first year from seed.* The skin is a beautiful silvery white; the flesh is snowy white, and of *particularly mild* and *pleasant flavor.* So sweet and tender is the flesh that it can be eaten raw, like an apple. The Silver King matures early and is uniformly of large size and perfect form.

MAMMOTH POMPEII.

This is another new Italian onion, of colossal proportions, having obtained the weight of over four pounds the first year from seed. Of round, flattened form but thick through, with reddish-brown skin and white flesh, of very mild flavor.

ONION SETS.

HOW TO GROW AND STORE THEM.

While it does not pay to raise onion sets for the purpose of growing onions, as they can be raised so much more cheaply directly from the black seed, yet, raised as a crop to be sold for the use of small gardeners, they are quite profitable if well managed. The same directions given in the preceding essays apply equally to growing the crop of sets, in the selection of the situation and quality of the soil. It is not, however, necessary to manure the ground so heavily for young sets—as quantity, not size, is the result to be obtained. The sets should average only about one half-inch in diameter. It is even more important in growing sets that the land be free from the seeds of all noxious weeds than in the crop of onions, as they stand so much more thickly upon the ground that it is almost impossible to pull grass or other tenacious weeds from among them without pulling the young bulbs also. If much weeding has to be done, it also greatly increases the expense, and conse-

63

quently lessens the profit. The amount of labor
and manure it takes to grow a crop of sets must
be carefully considered in relation to the profits.
With the expense for the large quantity of seed
required the margin for profit is very small, unless
the crop raised be a large one, and hence care and
constant watchfulness should be exercised to make
it profitable with the least expenditure of labor.
In no case is the time-honored maxim "that a
stitch in time saves nine" more applicable than
in killing the weeds the instant they appear, or
to prevent their appearance by frequent cultivation.

In growing sets on new ground (that is, ground
that has not previously been planted in onions)
they are more easily handled in following on
ground that has been planted in some root crop,
such as turnips or beets, as these leave the ground
clean from weeds and litter and in a fine, friable
condition. Where long, coarse manure is to be
applied, it should be put on the fall previous and
plowed well under, cross plowing in the spring
to bring it up and have it mix thoroughly in the
surface soil. If compost or commercial fertilizers
are to be used, plow the ground in the fall and
cross plow in the spring; then, as soon as the plowing is done, apply the fertilizer, harrow and cultivate the soil into the finest possible condition. If
this cannot be accomplished with the cultivator
and plow, then the plot must be gone over with a
sharp steel rake where each row is to stand. A

better way, where the rows are to be planted closely, is to rake in windrows every six feet and then gather up and remove all the stones, sticks, etc., gathered by the rakes.

Where the crop is to be worked with wheel hoes the rows may be sowed as closely as fourteen inches apart, but we prefer to sow in broad drills, two to three inches wide and two and a half to three feet apart, or as closely as it is possible to cultivate them without throwing dirt upon the young sets. The cultivator used for this purpose should have the teeth plates narrow, not over one and a half inches in breadth, so as to work the soil up loose and fine and not throw up ridges of dirt to smother the young sets; the narrower the blade of the cultivator hoe is, the nearer is it safe to work, thus diminishing the hand labor to be performed. In laying out the rows for sowing, a marker should be used, so as to get them at perfectly equal distances apart, teeth being set in a piece of scantling for this purpose, at the proper distances apart for the rows, and a handle attached to pull it by. The first row is marked with the outside tooth against the line, afterward it tracks in the last row marked out. Where the seed is to be sown by hand, as is most frequently done, the teeth should be an inch and one-half or more in width and blunt pointed; then, if the head piece or scantling is heavily weighted, it will make the drills all ready for sowing. Where a drill or sower is used, the marker should have small, sharp teeth,

5

and be drawn lightly over the soil, just making a guide for the drill to follow. For sowing the seed by hand we would recommend the use of a small tin box, such as a baking-powder can, the diameter of which is the same as the width of the drill to be planted. The bottom of this is perforated with holes slightly larger than the diameter of the onion seed, but not large enough to allow two seeds to pass through the same hole at once. By filling this and lightly shaking it along the drill, it will sow very quickly and evenly. When the end of the row is reached, the sower, on his knees, travels back along the row, carefully covering in the fine soil with both hands; the depth is, of course, regulated in working the drills, and should vary from a scant half-inch in the heavy soils to a full inch in the lightest loam. The rows should be firmed with a light hand roller when planted.

While it is not so important to get the crop in at the very earliest time possible, we would recommend plowing the whole plot at one time, but only preparing for sowing so much of the plot as can be sown in one day to prevent drying out.

VARIETIES AND AMOUNT OF SEED TO BE SOWN.

Only four varieties of onions are generally used for growing sets, namely: EXTRA EARLY RED, YELLOW DUTCH or STRASBURG, YELLOW DANVERS and WHITE PORTUGAL or SILVER SKIN, the two latter being mainly grown. The RED WETHERSFIELD, which is much grown for bulbs, is too strong growing to form marketable sets; besides, it so easily matures onions from the seed that there would be no object in raising and keeping over the sets, not to speak of the danger of its running to seed if treated in this manner. This applies also to the Italian varieties, which produce onions of immense size from seed.

For the purpose of raising sets, we would recommend the sowing of not less than fifty to sixty pounds of seed to the acre; and if the exact size of the plot is not known, would suggest that a piece of ground two hundred and eight feet on each side contains one acre. This can be quickly estimated by counting the panels of the fence, which, ordinarily, are ten feet in length.

In cultivating and weeding, the same directions given in the Essays apply, excepting that the sets are not thinned. They should stand so thickly in the row as to touch each other when ripe, but not so thickly as to cause them to become misshapen.

When the sets have attained their growth and begin to ripen off, the maturing can be facilitated by rolling an empty barrel over the rows, mashing the green tops. This checks the flow of sap to the tops and tends to hasten the ripening.

In gathering the sets loosen them with a sharp steel rake, getting the teeth well *under* the bulbs, and rake lightly into windrows, rolling them over and over as much as possible to cleanse from any adhering soil. If it is a dry time, they should be left in the windrows (not over two inches in depth) to sweat for a few days. Then gather up and spread them two inches thick on the floor of a cool loft or barn, or stack them in crates, as hereafter described.

MANUFACTURE OF STORAGE CRATES.

Crates can be made very cheaply, last a great many years if carefully handled, and will more than repay the cost of material and construction in a single season. They admit of storing large quantities of sets in the smallest possible space, and allow the air to circulate freely through all parts of the stack. The materials used in their construction are roofing lath one by two and a half inches, and plastering lath, which come four feet in length, one inch wide and half an inch thick. Of the roofing lath, make a square frame measuring four feet from outside to outside one way and six feet the other way. This is nailed together the flat way of the stuff, the width of the pieces making the sides of the crate; a brace of the same stuff is nailed in the middle to further stiffen this frame; in a six-foot crate this should be the long way of the crate, so as to relieve the strain on the bottom. Nail all the corners as solidly as possible with ten-penny nails. Then laying this frame on the floor, cover one side of it with the plastering lath to form a bottom. Nail these on firmly with four-penny

nails to the sides and to the center brace, leaving
a space of about half an inch between the laths;
this is readily done by standing a lath up on edge
close against the one just nailed and then nailing
the next against the one on edge, which can then
be pulled out, leaving the proper space for ventilation. The sets are placed in these crates to the
depth of two inches, and the crates are then piled
one above another to the height of the room,
pieces of the roofing lath being laid on each crate
as it is put up, to make a two-inch air passage
between the layer of sets in the one just stacked
and the slatted bottom of the one above. The
bottom crate should be raised at least four inches
above the floor, not only to insure a good circulation of air, but also to allow the cats free passage
to every part of the floor in pursuit of mice. We
have been thus particular in the description of
these crates, as the storing and wintering of the
sets are matters of equal importance with the
growing of them. Unless these details are carefully attended to, the grower may suffer the loss
of the whole crop stored; either from rotting,
if a free circulation of air is not kept up, or
from sprouting, if kept too warm. The loft or
storage room should have ventilators or windows at each end, and should have constant care
to keep them well aired and the temperature as
dry and cool as possible, just so that they do not
freeze. In a large loft where they are kept over
winter there should be stoves to maintain a low

fire on nights when there is great danger of freezing, but where these are used the crates should not be stacked within several feet of them, or the nearest ones will sprout and become worthless. Even when the fires are lighted, air must be admitted and the temperature kept as near the freezing point as possible. The necessity for firing can be largely done away with by fitting windows, ventilators and all cracks with strips of listing. We would also recommend these instructions for storing and wintering the sets to the attention of the onion grower, as we believe it to be the best and surest manner of wintering the onion crop.

It has also the great advantage over other methods of enabling the grower to market or ship all or any part of his crop at a moment's notice, thus being able to take advantage of any scarcity or rise in the market. Where the crates are not at hand, the sets may be wintered by leaving them in piles six to twelve inches deep on the floor, and covering them with successive layers of hay as the weather goes down below the freezing point; but, though we have known this to be successfully done, it requires a great deal of judgment, and we would advise all who have not the crates and storage facilities to sell their crop to the large dealers who make a business of handling them as soon as they are cleaned and sorted. Even if the price realized is not so large, "the bird in the hand is much safer than the two in the bush."

CLEANING AND SORTING.

This is to be done the first opportunity after they are thoroughly dried, but if they are to be carried through the winter, we would leave them in the crates till winter, when the hands can be profitably employed in this work without interfering with other farm work, one crate being emptied by each pair of hands, and, as cleaned, sorted into another. The cleaning is done by rubbing them around and pulling off with the fingers all tops and roots that do not separate from the bulbs when they are gently rubbed against each other and the slatted bottom of the crate. The sorting is quickly performed by running them through a grain fan sieve, or other sieve having meshes three-quarters of an inch in diameter. Those which will not pass through are too large for sets, grade as pickling onions, and can be sold to pickle factories.

Horticultural Books.

WHY WE PUBLISH THEM.

In the success of the planter is the germ of our success. To help to this, we publish at merely nominal prices books giving the plainly told practice of accepted experts in gardening. This idea has proven wonderfully attractive, and from a modest beginning this feature of our business has grown to very considerable proportions, editions of 20,000 copies not being unusual.

We trust the following pages, on which we describe the different works issued up to date, will interest all progressive planters, from the woman who desires to beautify the home garden, to the man who grows a thousand acres.

At the prices named, we will send the books, postpaid, direct, or they may be had through any book store in the United States.

W. Atlee Burpee & Co., Philadelphia.

Specimen illustration from the book.

THE BEAUTIFUL FLOWER GARDEN.

BY THE WELL-KNOWN BOSTON ARTIST,
F. SCHUYLER MATHEWS,
IN COLLABORATION WITH ARTHUR FEWKS,
OF NEWTON HIGHLANDS, MASS.

We are confident this new book will mark an epoch in artistic flower-gardening, to which people everywhere are turning such close attention. Art is simple and natural;—yet where is a teacher more needed than in simple, natural arrangement? There are many gardens laid out with evident care, yet even in these it must be admitted that something is lacking, and MR. MATHEWS says, "all will agree with me that this something is *art* in gardening." Who is better able to tell us what properly pertains to the subject than a trained artist who is also an enthusiastic amateur gardener? The pages are literally overflowing with pen-and-ink sketches made from nature, so that the veriest novice may easily learn to arrange plants and flowers harmoniously. The artist-author has drawn from the best in the artistic world of gardening, showing the influence of the formal English style, also that of the Italian renaissance period, not overlooking the influence exerted by the Japanese, who are a wonderfully artistic people.

Above everything, harmony should rule in the garden; all nature proclaims the principle: "art itself is nature." Therefore, the most elaborative attention is given by the author to making plain the principles of harmony.

Not the least important part of this valuable book is that devoted to the careful description of flowers which may be easily procured and grown from seeds, bulbs, and cuttings. Bright sketches show the form and habit of growth of each class. The closing chapters are devoted to careful cultural directions by ARTHUR FEWKS, a professional grower of wide reputation. All the works previously published on this subject are elaborate and expensive, treating for the most part of the management of great estates and parks; this book is for the million seeking to surround their homes with nature in her charming moods. We therefore consider it to our interest to make the price actually less than the cost per copy for the first edition.

Finely illustrated, and in handsomely designed covers.
Price 50 cts., postpaid.

CAN BE ORDERED FROM THE PUBLISHERS, OR
ANY BOOK STORE IN THE UNITED STATES.

Published by W. ATLEE BURPEE & CO., Philadelphia, Pa.

INJURIOUS INSECTS

AND THE USE OF INSECTICIDES.

A NEW BOOK.

By FRANK W. SEMPERS,

**Director of Fordhook Chemical Laboratory; author of MANURES:
How to Make and How to Use Them.**

A very complete and convenient treatise on insects destructive to Fruit, Field, and Garden crops. Contains the latest and best methods for preventing insect injuries and gives reliable formulas for making insecticides. This book is plainly written for the million, and is filled with life-like illustrations which will greatly aid the farmer in identifying his insect foes.

SYNOPSIS OF THE CONTENTS: — Natural and Artificial Methods of Destroying Insects—Insecticides, with Full Directions for Making and Using Them — Insects Injurious to Orchard and Garden Fruits — Insects Destructive to Vegetable Crops and to Grains and Grasses — Those which Annoy Domestic Animals —Insects of the Household.

A book badly needed by every one who has a Farm or Garden.

PRICE, POSTPAID, 50 CENTS.

CAN BE ORDERED FROM THE PUBLISHERS, OR
ANY BOOK STORE IN THE UNITED STATES.

PUBLISHED BY

W. ATLEE BURPEE & CO., PHILADELPHIA, PA.

ONIONS FOR PROFIT.

A Full and Complete Hand-Book of Onion Growing.

At last we publish a really complete hand-book on Onion grow-ing, the first ever issued ; it is by MR. T. GREINER, the author of the NEW ONION CULTURE, of which book he says : "The NEW ONION CULTURE was intended mostly to present a new phase of the business, and to encourage further researches in an entirely new direction. As a 'Hand-book of Onion Growing' it has short-comings and is far from being complete. It leaves too much room for per-sonal inquiries. I have looked the field of horti-cultural literature in America over pretty closely, and am unable to find a hand-book for the Onion grower the teach-ings of which are based on modern methods and embody (as they should in order to justify any claims of being 'up-to-the-times') the two meth-ods, the old and the new, in profitable combina-tion."

There is Big Money

in Onions : $500, and even more, per acre, if you know how to get it out. This money is for the "up-to-the-times" market gardener, the progres-sive farmer, and the bright farmer's boy everywhere. No more practical and successful Onion grower than Mr. Greiner can be found, and he gives his latest knowledge in ONIONS FOR PROFIT without reserve. The book will undoubtedly mark an epoch in works on this subject.

Every reasonable question as to Onion growing is answered in its over one hundred pages, which are enlivened with fully fifty illustrations prepared for this book, making it handsome as well as valuable.

Price, Postpaid, 50 Cents,

CAN BE ORDERED FROM THE PUBLISHERS, OR
ANY BOOK STORE IN THE UNITED STATES.

PUBLISHED BY

W. ATLEE BURPEE & CO., PHILADELPHIA, PA.

CELERY FOR PROFIT.

All agree that Celery offers greater chances for making money than any other garden crop. The difficulties encountered by the old methods of growing, however, made success uncertain, and sure only with comparatively few expert growers. Modern methods make all this uncertainty a thing of the past. From the same area which would give $100.00 in any other vegetable, you

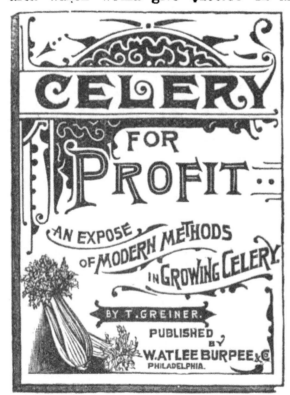

may take $400.00 or even $500.00 in Celery, if you **know how.** This new book, just published, is written by T. GREINER, author of ONIONS FOR PROFIT, and other books on gardening. It tells how to dispense with nine-tenths of the labor generally thought necessary in Celery growing, and how to make the business pay really big profits. Under the right culture and conditions several thousand dollars' worth of Celery can be raised on a single acre. The book is thoroughly complete in every detail, and is embellished with many helpful and original illustrations. Here is a glimpse of the table of contents :—

Generalities—An Introduction—The Early Celery—The New Celery Culture—The Irrigation Problem—The Fall and Winter Crop—Winter Storage—Marketing Problems—Varieties, etc., etc.

Price, Postpaid, 30 Cents,

CAN BE ORDERED FROM THE PUBLISHERS, OR ANY BOOK STORE IN THE UNITED STATES.

PUBLISHED BY
W. ATLEE BURPEE & CO., PHILADELPHIA, PA.

SELECTION IN SEED GROWING.

IS an interesting and instructive book of 112 pages, illustrated, giving the vital principles which underlie the growing of vegetables, flowers, or grains from seed. It tells how new varieties are obtained and developed, and gives in full the important essays on this subject read before the World's Horticultural Congress, Chicago, with the views of such leading European authorities as M. de Vilmorin, of Paris; Mr. Pedersen - Bjergaard, of Copenhagen, and Dr. Wittmack, of Berlin; including essays and discussions by such well-known American horticulturists and seed growers as Messrs. Morse, Allen, Hill, Craig, McMillan, Garfield, Burpee, Prof. Trelease, and Prof. Bailey. The book

gives in detail the **Modern Methods of the Seed Trade**, with illustrations of the practical work in seed growing and seed testing at Fordhook Farm.

Price, Postpaid, 10 Cents.

CAN BE ORDERED FROM THE PUBLISHERS, OR
ANY BOOK STORE IN THE UNITED STATES.

PUBLISHED BY

W. ATLEE BURPEE & CO., PHILADELPHIA, PA.

Our Catalogues, Published Annually, are:

BURPEE'S FARM ANNUAL. This is the foundation. See next page.

Special Advertisement of BURPEE'S SEEDS. This is an abridged catalogue, descriptive mostly of our Novelties, which is mailed to those names on our books from whom, for one reason or another, we did not receive an order the previous season. It is an invitation to apply for our FARM ANNUAL, if the recipient is still in need of seeds,—the FARM ANNUAL being too expensive to mail broadcast unless it is actually wanted.

Illustrated Circular of UNTRIED NOVELTIES. See synopsis given on page 35. Issued January 15th, and mailed to our customers free on application.

BURPEE'S BLUE LIST. Special price list of SEEDS IN BULK for market gardeners and florists who have occasion to purchase in large quantities. Mailed to the secretary of any Farmers' Club, Market Gardener, or Florist on application.

BURPEE'S RED LIST. This is a WHOLESALE PRICE LIST OF SEEDS for dealers only. In response to numerous inquiries, we would state emphatically that we never send out boxes of seeds to be sold on commission, but supply first-class seeds to dealers willing to pay a fair price for them. This catalogue is sent only to *bona fide* dealers in seeds.

BURPEE'S MANUAL OF THOROUGHBRED LIVE STOCK. This is issued in January of each year, and is a most complete illustrated catalogue of THOROUGHBRED SHEEP, SWINE, FANCY POULTRY, and ROUGH-COATED SCOTCH COLLIE DOGS. It is sent without request to all live-stock customers of the previous year, and is mailed to all others **FREE on application.** Every Stock Breeder, Poultry Fancier, and all Farmers interested in improved stock *should write for it.* The many Illustrations are accurately engraved from nature, and the merits of the different breeds are fairly presented. If you want a copy, send a postal card asking for the "ILLUSTRATED MANUAL OF THOROUGHBRED LIVE STOCK."

FORDHOOK COLLIE KENNELS. This is the title of a special illustrated folio of SCOTCH COLLIES, as bred at FORDHOOK FARM, with photogravure illustrations and much interesting information. Mailed in a circular tube on receipt of a two-cent postage stamp.

BURPEE'S CATALOGUE OF FLOWERING BULBS, PLANTS, AND SEEDS FOR AUTUMN PLANTING. A complete illustrated catalogue of Hyacinths, Tulips, Crocus, and other bulbs and flower roots for winter blooming and fall planting; also embracing seasonable seeds and plants. Issued September 1st of each year. Free on application.

W. ATLEE BURPEE & CO., PHILADELPHIA, PA.

Printed in Great Britain
by Amazon

62970073R00051